CHINA CONNECTION

FINDING ANCESTRAL ROOTS

FOR CHINESE IN AMERICA

CHINA CONNECTION

Finding Ancestral Roots for Chinese in America

BY

JEANIE W. CHOOEY LOW

黄育貞

Calligraphy and Illustrations

JWC LOW COMPANY - SAN FRANCISCO

CHINA CONNECTION

JWC LOW COMPANY
P.O. Box 472012
San Francisco, CA. 94147

For the "Unsung Heroes" in Our Families

It's the bits and pieces which make up the whole story!

CONTENTS

CONTENTS (CONT'D)

CONTENTS (CONT'D)

FOREWORD

I started writing this book while waiting for government records on my father. Many friends wanting to do their own family history asked for written instructions. In this book, I have attempted to outline some of the resources available to English speakers or those with limited bilingual skills to access family records, such as the Angel Island immigration papers.

I've come to learn that many older immigrants do not want to discuss their immigration experiences even with their own families. So, I've included some historical background discussion on the following topics: Chinese immigration; "Paper Names"; "Amnesty" program; composites of case numbers, and gravestone inscriptions. My bibliography lists books which offer more comprehensive discussions on the Chinese in America.

I think anyone can do their family research with some enthusiasm, time, patience, and an intriguing mind. There are many family stories sitting on library shelves or in some dusty drawer waiting for discovery.

I learned that my family's earliest connection with the United States was an ancestor who came by ship to mine gold and helped build the transcontinental railroad, before retiring in China. Another branch of my family had a carpentry business in San Francisco, Chinatown which helped to rebuild Chinatown after the San Francisco 1906 earthquake and fire.

I was born in the United States, and I have always felt very connected to my Chinese roots through my parents. They taught my siblings and myself the language and cultural traditions of their country.

This book is not intended to be the absolute word regarding Chinese-American ancestral roots. Information is periodically being uncovered, still other sources are not indexed. I apologize for any mistakes the reader may encounter.

Good Luck in your search!

Jeanie W. Chooey Low
February 10, 1994
Revised Second Edition

x

ACKNOWLEDGEMENTS

I am deeply indebted to my relatives and friends who discussed their immigration experiences and family stories. Many encouraged me to write this resource for their children and those interested in Chinese Americans.

The author expresses her appreciation and gratitude to the many professionals in the fields of library science, archives, Asian studies, history, education, genealogy, and publishing who offered their observations and encouragement in the creation of this work. I bow to those researchers and historians who laid the groundwork for the Asian Studies field.

Special thanks to: Neil Thomsen, National Archives-Pacific Sierra Region; Archivists of the National Archives regions; Waverly Lowell, Pacific Sierra; Margaret Hacker, Southwest; Robert Morris, Northeast; MidAtlantic; Pacific Northwest; and Pacific Southwest; Paul Chow, Angel Island Immigration Station Foundation and volunteer at the National Archives-Pacific Sierra Region.

The Chinese Historical Society of America and Asian American Studies, San Francisco State University for sponsoring the "The Repeal and Its Legacy", A conference on the 50th Anniversary of the Repeal of the Chinese Exclusion Acts, November 12-14, 1993 of which I was a panelist.

The late, Rev. Taam Tso Tin, "T.T.", Chinese Methodist Church, and Principal of Hip Wo Chinese Academy for giving young Chinese-Americans a sense of belonging. The late, Katharine Pedley, Librarian, City College of San Francisco for her encouragement.

I am also indebted to my husband, Steve and my children, Eric and Janine for their energy in helping to produce the second edition.

My parents for immigrating to the United States. I thank my Mother for additional translations and the cover photo. My sister, Linda Ching Wong and Marian Gan Gresham for marketing expertise; and Eileen Lo for computer typesetting expertise.

Let's start at the beginning ...

INTRODUCTION

Chinese Americans look to the past to assess their achievements in the United States and identities. The history of the United States is dotted with influences from the early Chinese immigrants. For example, Chinese first came as diplomats, merchants, seamen, scholars, and laborers. The latter group worked in agriculture, built wineries, land reclamation, developed the oyster industry, domestic service, cigar and woolen factories, and helped build the transcontinental railroad.

The largest group of Chinese came from Guangdong province in China when gold was discovered in California in 1848. By following the turmoil in China and economic opportunities in the world, we can see other factors why the Chinese immigrated to all the parts of the globe. (Table 1).

There were major wars and internal struggle to gain territorial rights and power within China. As a result of being conquered by foreign world power, many Chinese ports were open to economic opportunities abroad.

During wars in China, men and boys were conscripted into battle, leaving women, children, and old people to fend for themselves. As a result, the land laid unattended, caused famines and bandits to prey on the villages. Many Chinese families chose to send their young men and boys abroad to the challenge of economic opportunities rather than conditions of turmoil at home.

CHINA CONNECTION

The mode of immigration, anti-Chinese exclusion laws, and wars caused the separation of families for years. In some cases, young men could not return home until the exclusion immigration laws were repealed decades later when they were old men.

The importance of searching for family records will often uncover these "unsung heroes" in our own families. Chinese in the United States can be proud of their humble beginnings. Researching your family history may take a span of months or years, but the rewards are monumental. The search for family roots may also take you to every corner of the world. For instance, Chinese also settled in Australia, Canada, Cuba, Germany, Great Britain, Holland, Malaysia, Philippines, Singapore, Trinidad, and Vietnam.

This book will guide your search from the United States back to your Chinese ancestral roots. I have listed some resources available and their procedures. In addition, I have also listed additional bibliographical resources at the end of the book which include many interesting stories of individual families.

INTERVIEW FAMILY MEMBERS

Before starting the search for family records, interview the older members of your family. As more generations pass, more of your family's history will be lost through assimilation by interracial marriages, loss of ethnic culture, language, and memory. However, patience and analysis is the key to interviewing older members of the family. Be aware that members of the family may have different versions of their family history. Family details may be verified with available documents, family records, or with other relatives. Other relatives may not want to discuss your family's beginnings, and you can only respect their privacy.

A relative may have already done the family history or be able to provide you with actual documents, such as: letters from relatives in China with the return address, photographs, ship tickets, citizen certificates, autobiographical audio or written material of family members, names of family in Chinese, or the location of the ancestral home. These will be valuable sources in putting your family's history together.

It may take several conversations with each relative before they remember more details. It would be helpful to tape record the interview and have a separate file for each relative. Send a family history questionnaire to gather information from relatives who live away. The questionnaire will encourage relatives to remember details. (Illus. 7).

In analyzing information from your family, several things must be kept in mind. For example, they may be talking about events which took place before the nineteenth century when parts of China were not developed, and the status of women were given a low priority. For instance, women were not usually the first of their families to immigrate. Men in China were given first priority in all aspects of life. Women were chosen by their future husbands, or their husband's family as wives and concubines without any courting period. Other women were often sold into prostitution and domestic service.

When older relatives talk about transportation in China, they may be talking about sedan chairs. For your understanding, each sedan seated only one person with two to four carriers. When individuals left their villages to immigrate to other countries, it was customary to have a procession of relatives accompany them to the ports of departure. During war years, developed roads were purposefully ruined by local people to prevent the advancement of enemy forces into the villages.

It is important to understand that there were other periods of gold discoveries, and other branches of the transcontinental railroad being built throughout the United States. (Table 1). Afterwards, Chinese started working as laborers on farms. As a result of the Civil War, opportunities also opened for Chinese laborers on Southern plantations and industries supplying the war effort.

In locating ancestors who immigrated, other factors which may be important are that some of the ships sunk in transit and many lives were lost. Other ancestors may have died while working on the railroads, gold fields, illness, suicide, or violence towards the Chinese. Their burial places may have been unmarked or they were buried at sea. (Table 3).

There is also the mention in families in the Guangdong province of the widespread adoption of young boys from other less fortunate families. Perhaps, the difficulties of returning from the United States or abroad and immigration policies for the men necessitated this practice. Those young boys later immigrated to the United States and elsewhere as teenagers to join their adoptive fathers in the family business. It is important to remember the opportunity afforded those individuals. The immigration records found may be the beginning of the family history for the descendants of those families.

Unfortunately, the true family of those adopted individuals may be difficult to trace because there were no formal papers for those adoptions. Often, those individuals were too young to remember their true surnames and villages. The adoption of those individuals may never be uncovered unless they discuss their experiences with their families.

"PAPER NAMES"

When the United States Government passed various Chinese exclusion acts from 1882 to 1924, many immigrants obtained a "paper name" to gain entry into the United States. The Chinese Exclusion Act of 1882 limited immigration into the United States to diplomats, students, merchants, and tourists.

The Chinese Exclusion laws were later to affect all Asians. They stopped the immigration of Chinese laborers for ten years. The Chinese immigration exclusion laws were passed because of the fear that the Chinese immigrants were outnumbering white laborers. These exclusion laws were finally repealed in 1943. Other discrimination laws denied Chinese immigrants of naturalization, owning property, and employment.

"Paper names" were created after the San Francisco earthquake and fire of 1906 destroyed most of the official birth records. For example, a Chinese citizen of the United States returning from a visit to his family in China would claim that a child was born to him there. The birth was registered when he returned to the United States to hold an approved entry space for his child, or he could sell the papers. Other Chinese obtained names from other countries and entered as Mexicans, Filipinos, and Japanese.

During the mid 1950's, there were widespread rumors and news that the United States Government sent immigration agents into the various Chinatowns to question residents to find residents with "paper names" for deportation. Those who arranged the "paper names" papers were imprisoned. This system of government investigation caused fear and suspicion within the Chinese community which prevails today.

During the 1960's, there was an amnesty program for those who came forward to confess to the use of a "paper name" and to claim their true names. Those individuals were granted immunity from deportation and lost their United States citizen status. To regain their citizenship, they waited five years as permanent resident aliens and underwent security checks and detailed interviewing before being eligible to take the citizenship examinations.

In 1957, a law was passed which would not deport any "paper name" individuals if their spouse, parent, or child was a United States citizen or permanent resident. Individuals born in the United States are automatically categorized as American citizens.

ANGEL ISLAND

In 1910, the U.S. Government established an immigrant detention center at Angel Island, California to initially process Chinese and later, Japanese, Filipino, and Korean immigrants. Immigrant procedures took anywhere from one week to two years before the immigrants were either granted Certificates of Identity Cards and approved for landing at San Francisco or deported. Photos were taken and medical examinations were administered on the new immigrants.

While waiting for the interview process with immigration inspectors, Chinese immigrants were detained in wooden dormitories at Angel Island. Families were separated, men and boys in the men's dormitory, and women and girls in the women's dormitory. Each dormitory held rows of metal bunks three tiers tall. Detainees felt like prisoners because they were only allowed outdoors at certain times. In addition, there were two locked gates before reaching the dining hall. There was a detention room for those who made trouble. Laundry was done by hand and hung next to each person's bunk. Many detainees wrote or carved poems on the walls of the dormitories to express their emotions of being detained in the wooden house.

There were detailed interrogation questions to administer the Chinese Exclusion laws. Immigrants were deported if their answers did not correspond to information the Government had from other immigrants from the same village and family members. There was an average of one hundred fifty questions asked of each immigrant. If the answers were not satisfactory, the immigrant was subjected to a second or third interrogation session. In addition, each immigrant was required to have witnesses who were also extensively questioned.

Fortunately, many of the immigrants were afforded habeas corpus court appeals through their attorneys and gained entry into the United States. Angel Island was closed in December, 1940 after a fire. However, until 1952, Chinese immigrants were still detained and questioned at various locations in San Francisco. (Table 1). From 1952 on, immigrants were processed from the ports of embarkation.

NATIONAL ARCHIVES

The repository of all released government records are housed by the National Archives in different regions of the United States. Of particular genealogical interest to Chinese are the immigration and naturalization records, selective service and census records. Records are from district or circuit courts where naturalization applications were sent, deportation cases and naturalization certificates were issued. There are several branches throughout the United States. It is open to the public five days a week. (Resources: National Archives).

NATIONAL ARCHIVES - PACIFIC SIERRA REGION

At the National Archives - Pacific Sierra Region, located in San Bruno, California, you will find the following of particular interest: immigrant files with English translations of questions and answers from Angel Island, 1910-1940 and Hawaii; Name index binders of Chinese immigrants passing through San Francisco, California and Hawaii; Microfiche passenger lists of vessels arriving at different U.S. ports, 1800-1957; Partnership lists for Chinese businesses in California, 1882-1950's; U.S. Census 1790-1920, Chinese Mortuary Records, San Francisco, and California 1870-1933, Chinese departure files, 1882-1913 on microfilm, and habeas corpus cases.

Most Chinese immigrants were processed for entry in the United States at Angel Island, California located west of San Francisco. Other entry ports were: Pt. Townsend (Seattle), Washington; Ellis Island, New York; San

Pedro, California; Galveston, Texas; and Hawaii.

However, in order to find documents on your family from governmental sources, you will need your relatives' name as spelled when immigrating, port of entry, and the date your relative entered the United States.

Before your visit to the National Archives - Pacific Sierra Region, telephone for an appointment to use the Certificate of Identity Name Index of Chinese Immigrants. You need a minimum of two hours for searching records. Researchers into the documents area are restricted to bring in only notebook paper and pencils. There is a locker for your other personal effects.

NATIONAL ARCHIVES - PACIFIC SIERRA:

NAME INDEX

After registering, ask for assistance in locating the Certificate of Identity Name Index Binders listing Asians processed through San Francisco, California; and Honolulu, Hawaii. These name indexes are not complete. They are limited to records released by the Immigration and Naturalization Department. Limited Chinese immigrant records before and after those dates may also be found at the National Archives.

CHINA CONNECTION

Many immigrants adopted English first names after they arrived in the United States. In searching an individual at the National Archives, start with the immigration name when he/she/they entered the United States.

Early immigrants of the 1860's had names which used "Ah" and their personal names, such as "Ah Sing". Family documents of immigrating families will be found under the husband's or father's name, or by individual names.

If the individual used a "paper name", search by the "paper name". An indication of a "paper name" would be the use of two different last names. If the exact spelling of the name is not known, try the different forms of spelling the name. For example, the name, "Choy, 蔡 ", is also spelled "Choi, Chooey, Toy, Tsai, and Tsoi". When immigrants applied for visas to the United States in Hong Kong, their surnames were transliterated into English from their spoken dialect resulting in the different spellings. The spelling ability and in some cases, the individual attitudes of investigators towards foreigners influenced the final spelling of the immigrant names.

When the individual's name is found in the Name Index, fill out a request form with the file numbers found next to the name listed. Each immigrant was given a file number derived from the number given to the ship and the passenger ticket. (Illus. 1). The clerk will retrieve the file from the storage area.

Each individual's folder may contain a photograph(s) of the person at the time of entry into the United States, photographs of the witnesses, questions and answers from Angel Island, Chinese wedding certificates, birth certificates, and other information related to the individual's acceptance or return to the United States. You may use a 35mm. camera to photograph the photos. Flash photography is not permitted to prevent further deterioration of the documents. Use 400 ASA, color or 1000 ASA, black and white speed film. The last page of the file lists each witness with their file number. (Illus. 2). Most often these witnesses were relatives, business associates, or "paper relatives". You may fill out request forms to see their files.

It should be noted that there may be other immigrants who will have a similar name as your relative. You will have to determine if you have the correct file judging from the entry date, photograph, and/or the applicant's name in Chinese. If your relative left and entered the United States a number of times, search by the last year of re-entry.

Please note that if your relative had a "paper name", the questions and answers from the immigration files were answers given as a member of the "paper family" and will not be your family history. However, it will give you an idea of the difficult process to immigrate into the United States at that time. The date of entry would be actual fact for family history and important if you would like a copy of the individual on the passenger list of the vessel recorded on microfiche.

CHINESE PASSENGER LISTS ON VESSELS

If your relative's name is not listed in the name index binders, you may search the person by microfilm as a passenger on the ship logs by date, ask for assistance. When you find the relative on the passenger list, turn to the date of arrival for his file number to retrieve the folder. (Illus. 1). You may make a copy of the microfilm on a duplication machine at the front desk.

However, if the relative's file folder is not found at the National Archives, it may be because the relative became a naturalized United States citizen or was a permanent resident. Those Angel Island records may be at the Federal Records Building (FRB) or may have been destroyed. The FRB is closed to the public. You may fill out a formal request for copies of those records kept at FRB to be released through the Freedom of Information and Privacy Act. Telephone the nearest United States Department of Justice-

Immigration and Naturalization Service for a form. (Resources).

FREEDOM OF INFORMATION AND PRIVACY ACT

NATURALIZED CITIZENS/

UNRELEASED IMMIGRATION RECORDS

Request the information for a naturalized citizen, a permanent resident, and other unreleased immigration records on the Freedom of Information/Privacy Act Request Form from the Department of Justice - Immigration and Naturalization Service Office. The request is sent to the district court where the individual's naturalization was finalized. In the case of a permanent resident, the request is sent to the local immigration and naturalization office.

The least expensive method of request for government records on an individual would be through the Privacy Act. The cost for requests filled out by the individual, his/her spouse or the Executor of the Estate is minimal.

However, if the individual is deceased and there is no other living relative, you may request the information under the Freedom of Information Act if you obtain the authorization or consent from the person's estate. You are charged research and duplication fees. The response time for the record is approximately two months to two years. Be sure to request copies of specific documents wanted, such as: Angel Island interview, photographs, or naturalization papers. You may also request an appointment for a personal inspection of the documents.

PARTNERSHIP LISTS OF CHINESE BUSINESSES IN CALIFORNIA, 1882 - 1950'S

Also, located at the National Archives - Pacific Sierra Region are records for Chinese business partnerships. From 1882 to the 1950's, the Department of Labor in Washington, D.C. required each Chinese mercantile business to furnish a list of all partners.

The list required each partner's name in English and Chinese, whether they were silent or active partners, the amount of interest they held in the firm, duties, addresses, and photos. Each file may contain original, handwritten Chinese documents. The immigration file number of each partner was listed and a picture of each managing member was posted in the file. These partnership lists are kept in a stack area at the archives and a request form is required. After perusing the business partnership list for your family's business, ask for your relative's file as listed on the reference sheet, if needed. (Illus. 3). In order to access business partnership files, you must know either the name of the business or its address(es).

Each business was inspected and witnesses interviewed to verify if the owners and their staff were merchants or laborers. During certain periods, if it could be proved that they were laborers, the United States would have reason to refuse re-entry to those individuals who had returned to China for business or a family visit. At other times, many partners were listed as having a thousand dollars invested in the business. Those amounts may have been borrowed to counteract a law in 1882 which stipulated that a returning Chinese laborer had to have assets or loans of $1,000, or family in the United States to re-enter. Later in 1888, another law refused re-entry to all returning laborers. (Table 1).

Among those cities in the San Francisco district were the following: Fresno, Gilroy, Isleton, Los Angeles, Marysville, Monterey, Merced, Newcastle, Oakland, Oroville, Pasadena, Red Bluff, Riverside, Sacramento, Salinas, San Bernadino, San Diego, San Francisco, San Jose, San Luis Obispo, San Rafael, Santa Barbara, Santa Cruz, Santa Rosa, Sebastopol, Stockton, and Watsonville. Limited out-of-state business records are also available if a merchant left or re-entered through San Francisco.

U.S. CENSUS 1790-1920

The census information at the National Archives are on microfiche. These will be actual records filled out on individual families who participated in the census surveys. There are some listings of Chinese in the census surveys.

In the California Census records of 1870, Chinese were listed in the early communities of: Alameda; Butte; Calaveras; Chico; Colusa; El Dorado; Humboldt; Kern; Los Angeles; Marin; Mariposa; Monterey; Nevada; Placer; Sacramento; San Joaquin; Santa Barbara; Santa Clara; Solano; Shasta; Siskiyou; Toulumne; Trinity; Tulare; Vacaville; and Yuba counties. These were many of the early goldminers, fishermen, and orchard workers.

The information found in the census are the names of each family member, age, birthplace, address, and occupation. However, bear in mind that information given may be incomplete because many Chinese families in the early nineteenth century may have been illiterate in English. Later, Chinese families with "paper names" may have shunned the collection of personal information for fear of deportation.

CHINESE MORTUARY RECORDS IN SAN FRANCISCO

AND CALIFORNIA, 1870 - 1933

These records were collected by the Department of Immigration and Naturalization Service for use in the prevention of identity forgeries. Of interest in the 1870's listings are individuals who died in their twenties and thirties of various ailments, such as: mining explosions, tuberculosis, opium smoking, hanging, venereal diseases, suicide, murder, railroad accidents, and unknown causes.

The occupations include miners, shoemakers, cooks, merchants, doctors, laundrymen, missionaries, cigar makers, ragpickers, actors, fishermen, firemen, butcher, gamblers, laborers, and prostitutes.

There are also those who died on the ships and in other states, such as: Alaska; Oregon; Helena, Montana Territory; Silver City; Idaho Territory (Idaho, Montana, and most of Wyoming); Utah; and Walla, Nevada. (Table 3).

If your efforts to find your relative's government records fail, ask for assistance from the Chinese Immigration Specialist at the National Archives. There are many microfilm sources, such as: Registers of Chinese Departing

CHINA CONNECTION

From and Returning to the U.S., October, 1882-October, 1908; Chinese Passenger Lists, 1897-1957; Register of Students Admitted under 4(e) Immigration Act of 1924, 1924-1946; Record of Natives Departing, 1909-1913; Register of Chinese Laborers Departing the U.S. 1882-1886 and other valuable microfilms.

If all the National Archives resources have been exhausted, you may want to pursue the community resources of family genealogy research in the sections below.

FAMILY BENEVOLENT ASSOCIATION

You may want to visit the family association if your relative was an active member. Someone there may be able to identify your family's ancestral lineage or know your family's historical roots in the United States. If your relative made a special donation, there may be an ancestral tablet, "sun gee pi" at the family association. Make a special appointment to see the ancestral tablet, and ask if there are any special donations required. You will need to speak Chinese or bring someone to act as your interpreter.

CEMETERIES

At first glance, cemeteries seem to be places of finality. However, Chinese cemeteries are bustling with activity twice a year. In the spring, there is "Ching Ming" and in the fall, there is the "Chung Yang" festival. During these times, families gather to officially care for the graves of their loved ones. There are ceremonial offerings of flowers, incense, food, and drink to the ancestors. It is also a time to renew family unity.

The practice of filial piety was prescribed by Confucius many centuries ago in China. If you have ever visited a Chinese cemetery, you will notice that the plots are located on hills or on mountain tops. In the United States, as in China, the location of a resting place is carefully chosen for the "Feng Shui" and its proximity to the heavens. From a practical point of view, the locations are good because of the excellent drainage. The gravestones are upright in keeping with the importance of honoring the deceased. Even today, there is a preference of the older immigrants to be buried among their fellow countrymen from their own districts on the hillsides in the Chinese cemeteries.

Gravestone memorials offer invaluable family history information especially if the inscriptions are in Chinese. The traditional Chinese gravestone is inscribed with the deceased person's name, birth and death date. It may also list information of the ancestral village, district, and province in China. (Illus. 3-6). It should be noted that an older relative who was born in the United States may list his ancestral home on the gravestone instead of his birthplace in the U.S. For example: " 香港人氏 ". (This person's family is from Hong Kong.)

Older gravestone dates reflect periods in Chinese government. The birth and death dates on the gravestones made reference to Chinese emperors: "T'ung Chih", 1862-1874; "Kuang Hsu", 1875-1908; and the Republic of China, 1912. For example, a death date stating the fifth year of the Republic of China which would translate to the approximate date of 1917 on the Gregorian calendar. (Table 2/Illus. 5). The month and date would follow the lunar calendar, ie; the "second month" might translate as March on the Gregorian calendar. During certain cycles, the lunar calendar would also reflect leap months and years.

In China, each person had as many as four names. It was customary for a person to have a birth name, school name, married name, and a respectful title when they died. If the individual was never married, the Chinese characters for "single woman, 花女" or "single man, 花仔" will be listed on the gravestone. (Illus. 4).

Many of the married women may only be identified by their maiden surnames. For example, on a gravestone, the woman's name might be listed **"Mrs. Wong, 黃夫人"** and the surname **"Chin 陳 "** and the word **"Shee, 氏 "** would follow. (Illus. 5). The **"Shee, 氏 "** character indicates that the woman's maiden name was **"Chin, 陳 "**. Until recently, little importance was given to the genealogy of Chinese women unless they were nobility or historically significant.

The stigma of using a "paper name" and assuming a "paper identity" is seen in the listing of two last names for some men on their stones, such as: listed in English, "Mr. Jung" and in Chinese, "Mr. Lee, 李 " (Illus. 6). The true name for this individual is "Lee". There are also examples in which the true family names are not included on the gravestones. The practice of omitting true family names will affect generations of their families to come. The amnesty program for "paper name" families meant possible deportation, loss of citizenship, and a "loss of face" in the American community. As a result, many "paper name" families chose not to apply for the amnesty program.

If you do not know the location of the grave, you will need to visit the cemetery association. The location of a grave in the Chinese cemetery will be listed by date of death, individual's Chinese name, and village at one of the Chinese cemetery associations.

When you visit the cemetery association, be sure to bring along a Chinese-speaking relative or interpreter if you do not speak Chinese. Also, bring the information of the deceased individual to the association. Each Chinese cemetery association maintains handwritten records in Chinese. Maps of the cemetery are available with section markers from each cemetery association. Western cemeteries list the location of the deceased by the date of death and person's name.

Before a trip to the cemetery to locate the gravestone, bring either a 35mm. camera, a calligrapher to copy the Chinese inscriptions on the stone, or stone rubbing materials. If you are photographing the inscriptions on the gravestone, be sure to have the inscriptions focused for legibility. You may wish to make a gravestone rubbing of the inscriptions. Tape a sheet of newsprint or thin paper over the inscriptions. Use the thick side of an unwrapped black crayon and gently rub it over the paper to get a clear picture.

FAMILY NAMES

The traditional Chinese name consists of three characters, such as " 謝 ⊗ ⊗ ." The first character, " 謝 ," is the family surname, the second, the generation name, and the third, the personal name. In some areas, the generation name is the last character.

The generation name was established by each family's founding fathers. They composed a family poem and each character signified a different generation. Individuals with the same generation name within each surname are not necessarily closely related. It only signifies that their birth level coincide.

In China, each surname family lived in the same village. Each village might consist of sixty to a hundred inhabitants. The generation name would be hung up at the bakery or butcher shop when wedding foods were distributed to close relatives.

In the United States, many landed immigrants later Americanized their surnames. Their work with American employers or acquaintances guided their choice of American names. Others, used their names as spelled at the time of immigration. Still others, maintained two names, one the "paper name", the other, the true name.

Some incorporated their true names as middle names while using the "paper name".

LIBRARIES: PUBLIC AND PRIVATE

Visit libraries with large Asian populations. There may be a large Asian studies collection. The reference librarians are very helpful in suggesting subject headings to locate books on Chinese in America; Chinese in Indonesia; Chinese in Mississippi, etc. Skim through the index of Chinese in America books for the mention of your relatives or the family business. Other books may not be indexed. These will require reading the material.

Ask if a map of districts or villages in China is available. These maps are sold in the Chinese bookstores. However, most available maps will list only the districts or county names and larger cities. It is preferable to have the map in Chinese because most place names have remained the same, and Chinese-speaking relatives can identify their villages in Chinese, whereas, there have been many different romanize spellings of place names.

After looking at the map, you may realize that before the twentieth century, travel in China was hampered by the great distances and rugged terrain before arriving at the ports of departure.

CHINA CONNECTION

Large city libraries may have newspapers on microfiche. Of interest to your family search would be the Name Index which list newspaper articles written about individuals or the obituary sections. Other sources available in libraries are the Special Collections and Archives. These departments may contain city blueprints of the old Chinatowns and photos of bygone eras.

TELEPHONE DIRECTORIES

Visit the city in which your relative resided. Check the telephone directory for its historical society and/or Chinese historical society, such as: in California: San Francisco, Locke, Napa, San Luis Obispo, Weaverwille, Denver, Colorado; New York; Oregon; Wyoming, etc. Large public libraries will have copies of neighboring county directories. Write or call for appointments with the archivist at the historical society.

GOVERNMENT RECORDS OF BUSINESS

If your family business was started by a relative, check to see if there are any documents with other relatives. You may also check with the tax collector's office for the founding date if available. The National Archives at the Pacific Sierra region in California has partnership lists of Chinese

businesses in San Francisco, and other businesses in California, 1882-1950's.
(Partnership Lists of Chinese Businesses).

VISIT CHINA

On a visit to China, you will want to make a trip to your ancestral home. Before visiting China, locate a map of the province, district, and village of your ancestral home. Bring the name of the ancestral village, names and photographs of your relatives written in Chinese. If there are relatives still living in China, they may be able to fill in the gaps in your family history. There may be portraits of the ancestors done in watercolors and hung in the family house.

Ancestral Halls

Ancestral worship in China was prescribed by the teachings of Confucius. Many families maintained an ancestral hall or room listing the male members and their spouses with their birth and death dates. Portraits of the ancestors were displayed in the hall. However, during the Chinese cultural revolution in the 1960's, most of the ancestral tablets, "sun gee pi" were confiscated and destroyed. Fortunately, in isolated sections of China, families who hid their ancestral tablets have them today. Other families have facsimiles of ancestral tablets on glass.

Pilgrimage

It is in China where you will make a pilgrimage into the mountains to visit the graves of your ancestors. Thoughts which may come to mind, may be about your family's sacrifices of separation for economic and academic opportunity in the United States and other parts of the world.

CONCLUSION

Occupations, such as "butcher, farmer, janitor, laundrymen, and seamstress," for many of the early Chinese immigrants may indicate that those individuals were peasants, uneducated and unskilled. However, many immigrants were craftsmen and educated. Some took menial jobs in the United States to feed their families. They filled valuable services needed in those early years of industry and new settlements. As a result of their humble beginnings and sacrifices in the United States, many of their descendants have become leaders in their fields. Family and honor is the driving force for Chinese.

CHINA CONNECTION

In the world, there is constant rivalry between geographically groups, each claiming to be culturally or academically superior. A valuable lesson is taught by the Chinese immigrant, any individual can aspire to any goal through persistence, hard work, and educational opportunities.

The treatment of the Chinese during earlier years of immigration surely produced a very cautious generation of Chinese-Americans. However, understanding their family immigration dilemmas will help free them and future generations.

Chinese-American women have especially reaped the rewards of immigration. Exposure of diverse cultures in the United States, education and the women's movement have improved their status.

It's Time to Start Your Family's Story!

Common Threads, One Spirit !

APPENDIX

1839-42	China loses the Opium War with Great Britain. Hong Kong given to Great Britain. Five Chinese ports open. Influx of missionaries into China.
1847	Three Chinese students brought into the United States by missionaries for educational study.
1847-74	Chinese laborers in Peru and Cuba.
1848	Gold discovered at Sutter's Mill, California. Merchants, laborers.
1851-64	Taiping Rebellion, China.
1852	Chinese in Australia for gold rush in South Wales and Victoria.
1858-60	More Chinese ports opened to foreign trade.
1858-59	Gold rush in Jefferson Territory (Colorado, parts of Kansas, New Mexico, Nebraska, and Utah).
1860	Gold discovered on Orofino Creek, Idaho.
1861-65	Civil War created labor opportunities for Chinese.
1862	Gold discovered in Boise Basin, Idaho.
1862-65	Gold discovered in Montana. (Grasshopper Creek, Bannock, Diamond City, and Virginia City).
1863	End of California Gold Rush.
1864-69	Chinese labor: Building the transcontinental railroad, agricultural labor, domestic service, mines, laundries, land reclamation, cigar and woolen factories.

TABLE 1 - TIME CHART AFFECTING CHINESE IMMIGRATION

1867-79	Pacific Mail Steamships Company established route between San Francisco, Yokohama, Shanghai, and Hong Kong.
1871-86	Anti-Chinese Acts of Violence: California, Colorado, Oregon, Wyoming, Washington.
1874-76	Gold discovered in South Dakota (Custer, Black Hills, Lead, and Deadwood).
1880-84	Canadian Pacific Railroad construction.
1880-86	U.S. eastern line of railroad construction.
1880's	Gold discovered in South Africa. Railroad development.
Late 1880's - Early 1900's	Chinese passengers arriving in San Francisco housed at a Pacific Mail Steamship Company shed for immigration processing.
1882-1943	U.S. Chinese Exclusion Laws.
1883	Northern Pacific Railroad crossed Montana.
1894-95	China at war with Japan.
1896	Alaska gold rush: Klondike region of the Yukon Territory.
1898	Chinese immigration to Hawaiian Islands prohibited.
1899	Gold discovered in Nome, Alaska.
1900	Boxer Rebellion in China.
1902	Gold discovered in Fairbanks, Alaska

TABLE 1 - TIME CHART AFFECTING CHINESE IMMIGRATION

1905-12	Democratic rebel attacks against the Manchu government. Republic of China established, 1912.
1906	San Francisco Earthquake and Fire: Lost of official birth records. Creation of "Paper Names".
1910-40	Angel Island as an Immigration Center.
1922	Chinese women denied entry into the U.S.
1923	Alaska railroad completed. Loss of U.S. citizenship as a result of marrying a non-citizen.
1930	Chinese wives allowed entry into the U.S. if they married an American citizen before May, 1924.
1931	Japanese invade Manchuria.
1934-35	Communist movement in China.
1937-45	War with Japan. World War II: Chinese in the U.S. serving in the military, ie, "Flying Tigers".
1941-42	Sharp Park, CA. Detention quarters for Chinese immigrants through San Francisco.
1943	Repeal of Chinese immigration exclusion laws.
1944-52	Chinese immigrants entering at San Francisco were detained at the Appraiser's Building at 630 Sansome Street, San Francisco.
1946	War Brides Act. Allowed wives and children of Chinese-American citizens to apply for citizenship. Husbands and children of female citizens were not admitted until 1952.

TABLE 1 - TIME CHART AFFECTING CHINESE IMMIGRATION

1949	Communist China. Chinese refugees in Hong Kong, United States, Canada, Great Britain & British Possessions, Australia.
1952	Immigration Processing done at ports of embarkation.
1953	Entry of refugees of Chinese revolution.
1955	Confessions of "Paper Names" sought and deportations resulted.
1957	No deportation of "paper name" individuals, if spouse or parent was a United States citizen, permanent resident alien, or if their children were born in the U.S.
1962	Hong Kong refugees permitted entry into the U.S. Amnesty for "Paper Names Confessions": Granted immunity from deportations, and lost their citizen status.
1965	Law which abolished the national origin quota system.
1966-70	Chinese Cultural Revolution: Most ancestral tablets destroyed.
1972	People's Republic improved relations with the West. Petitions available to bring relatives to the United States.

TABLE 1 - TIME CHART AFFECTING CHINESE IMMIGRATION

CHINESE DYNASTY

夏	Hsia	2205 - 1766 B.C.
商	Shang	1766 - 1122 B.C.
周	Chou	1122 - 256 B.C.
春秋	Spring & Autumn Annals	770 - 475 B.C.
戰國	Warring States	475 - 221 B.C.
秦	Ch'in	221 - 207 B.C.
漢	Han	206 B.C. - A.D. 220
三國	Three Kingdoms	A.D. 220 - 265
晉	Jin	A.D. 265 - 420
南北朝	Southern & Northern Dynasties	A.D. 420 - 589
隋	Sui	A.D. 581 - 618

TABLE 2 - CHINESE DYNASTIES

Chinese Dynasty (Cont'd)

唐	Tang	A.D. 618 - 907
五代十國	Five Dynasties & Ten Kingdoms	A.D. 907 - 979
宋	Sung	A.D. 960 - 1279
元	Yuan	A.D. 1271 - 1368

TABLE 2 - CHINESE DYNASTIES

明 朝   **MING DYNASTY**

洪武 Hung Wu		A.D. 1368 - 1398
建文 Chien Wen		A.D. 1399 - 1402
永樂 Yung Lo		A.D. 1403 - 1424
洪熙 Hung Hsi		A.D. 1425
宣德 Hsuan Teh		A.D. 1426 - 1435
正統 Cheng T'ung		A.D. 1436 - 1449
景泰 Ching T'ai		A.D. 1450 - 1456
天順 T'ien Shun		A.D. 1457 - 1464
成化 Ch'eng Hua		A.D. 1465 - 1487
弘治 Hung Chih		A.D. 1488 - 1505
正德 Cheng Teh		A.D. 1506 - 1521

TABLE 2 - CHINESE DYNASTIES

Ming Dynasty (Cont'd)

嘉靖 Chia Ching   A.D. 1522 - 1566

隆慶 Lung Ch'ing   A.D. 1567 - 1572

萬歷 Wan Li   A.D. 1573 - 1620

泰昌 T'ai Ch'ang   A.D. 1620

天啓 T'ien Ch'i   A.D. 1621 - 1627

崇禎 Ch'ung Cheng   A.D. 1628 - 1644

TABLE 2 - CHINESE DYNASTIES

清朝   **CH'ING DYNASTY**

順治 Shun Chih   A.D. 1644 - 1661

康熙 K'ang Hsi   A.D. 1662 - 1722

雍正 Yung Cheng   A.D. 1723 - 1735

乾隆 Ch'ien Lung   A.D. 1736 - 1795

嘉慶 Chia Ch'ing   A.D. 1796 - 1820

道光 Tao Kuang   A.D. 1821 - 1850

咸豐 Hsien Feng   A.D. 1851 - 1861

同治 T'ung Chih   A.D. 1862 - 1874

光緒 Kuang Hsu   A.D. 1875 - 1908

宣統 Hsuan T'ung   A.D. 1909 - 1911

TABLE 2 - CHINESE DYNASTIES

1870 - 1918	Microfilm handwritten English records of deceased Chinese listed by date of death. Vital statistics listed: name, age, occupation, place of death, birthplace, cause of death if known, undertaker, place of burial.
1874 - 1878	Among the records are listed approximately 790 boxes of Chinese deceased bones sent to San Francisco, CA. for re-internment at Laurel Hill Cemetery, City Cemetery, and Golden Gate Cemetery. The identity of these deceased are unknown. Death dates range from 1850-1878. Later, it was customary to have identified remains sent back to China. Since, 1950's, most immigrants buried in the U.S.
	The boxes of "Unknown Chinese bones" were sent from the following locations: California; Idaho Territory; Louisiana; Missouri; Nevada; Oregon; Pennsylvania; Utah Territory (parts of Nevada, Colorado and Wyoming); and British Columbia.
	Reports of ousting and anti-Chinese violence outside of San Francisco, CA. may have been the reason for the move of deceased remains.
1900	San Francisco, Board of Supervisors passed an ordinance to prohibit burials in the city limits after August 1, 1901.
1914	San Francisco, Board of Health sent out notices for the following cemeteries to relocate outside the city limits: Calvary, Masonic, Odd Fellow, and Laurel Hill. Chinese Cemetery at Laurel Hill later moved to Golden Gate Cemetery. Golden Gate Cemetery was later turned into use as a park. Other S.F. cemeteries relocated to Colma.
1918 - 1933	Chinese mortuary records for California. These are typed and generally alphabetized in English.

TABLE 3 - CHINESE MORTUARY RECORDS FOR SAN FRANCISCO AND CALIFORNIA, 1870-1933

CHINA CONNECTION

313175X   150   PORT OF SAN FRANCISCO   VESSEL: PRESIDENT JACKSON

MAY 28, 1934

SERIAL NO.	TICKET NO.	NAME	CLASS	RESIDENCE	REFER TO	DATE REFERRED	DATE RETURN	ADMITTED
	XI - 5	Lee, ---	Merchant	San Francisco				5/28/34
	X2 - 7	Wong,--- ---	Wife of Merchant	Sacramento				6/05/34
	X3 - 7	Kwan,------	Son of Son of Native	San Francisco				
	X3 - 8	Fong,--- ---	Laborer	Yreka				7/31/34
	X3 - 9	Wong,--- ---	Native	San Francisco				

FILE NUMBER FOR NAME INDEX AT NATIONAL ARCHIVES: 313175X -X3-9

DATE OF SHIP'S ARRIVAL AT PORT: MAY 28, 1934

DATE INDIVIDUAL'S PAPERS AND INTERVIEWS ENDORSED AND INDIVIDUAL ADMITTED TO U.S.

ILLUS. 1 - PASSENGER LIST, VESSEL, COMPOSITE

REFERENCE SHEET

NO. 313175X/ X 3-9

CASES USED IN CONNECTION WITH ABOVE CASE

NUMBER	NAME	STEAMER	DATE OF ARRIVAL	RELATIONSHIP
255566/ X 4-30	Wong, xx	Shinyo Maru	5/10/15	A1 Father
288300/ X 5-9	Wong, xx	Asia	1/31/16	A1 Uncle
387569/ X 9-7	Seto, xx	President Coolidge	6/06/25	Business Partner

ILLUS. 2 - REFERENCE SHEET OF WITNESSES, COMPOSITE

CHINESE Simple / Formal		ENGLISH
一 /	壹	1
二 /	貳	2
三 /	叄	3
四 /	肆	4
五 /	伍	5
六 /	陸	6
七 /	柒	7
八 /	捌	8
九 /	玖	9
零		0
十 /	拾	10

ILLUS. 3 - CHINESE NUMBERS, FORMS

CHINESE Simple / Formal	ENGLISH
二 十 ／ 廿	20
三 十 ／ 卅	30
一 百 ／ 佰	100
一 千 ／ 仟	1000
五 十 ／ 伍 拾	50, Position of number in front of 10 (Number multiply by 10)
十 七 ／	17, Position of numbers after 10 (10 + number)

ILLUS. 3 - CHINESE NUMBERS, FORMS

年	Year
月	Month
三月	March
五月	May
生於	Birth
終於	Passed away
西曆	Gregorian Calendar
縣	Name of County in China
村	Name xx Village within district
氏	Maiden name or origin is placed before character
歲	Age
仔	Single man
女	Single woman
花	
花	
夫人／門	Wife
黃夫人	Mrs. Wong/wife
生於一八八七年	Born in, 1887
終於一九七三年	Passed away 1973

ILLUS. 4 - KEY GRAVESTONE WORDS, U.S.

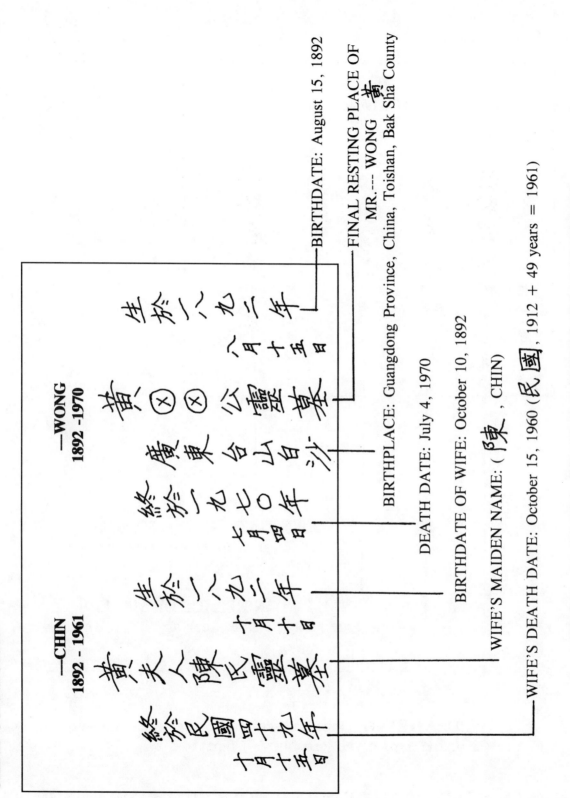

BIRTHDATE: August 15, 1892

FINAL RESTING PLACE OF
MR.--- WONG 黃
Guangdong Province, China, Toishan, Bak Sha County

BIRTHPLACE: Guangdong Province, China, Toishan, Bak Sha County

DEATH DATE: July 4, 1970

BIRTHDATE OF WIFE: October 10, 1892

WIFE'S MAIDEN NAME: (陳 , CHIN)

WIFE'S DEATH DATE: October 15, 1960 (民 國 , 1912 + 49 years = 1961)

ILLUS. 5 - GRAVESTONE, INSCRIPTIONS, COMPOSITE

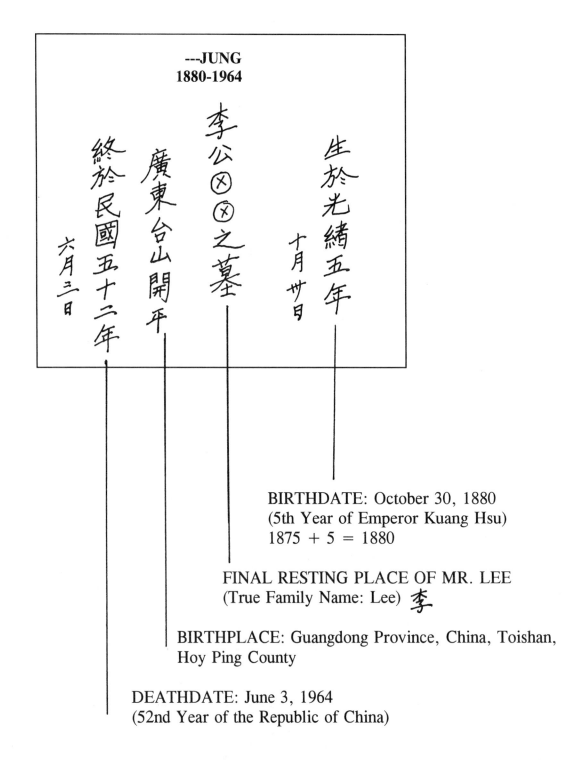

BIRTHDATE: October 30, 1880
(5th Year of Emperor Kuang Hsu)
1875 + 5 = 1880

FINAL RESTING PLACE OF MR. LEE
(True Family Name: Lee) 李

BIRTHPLACE: Guangdong Province, China, Toishan,
Hoy Ping County

DEATHDATE: June 3, 1964
(52nd Year of the Republic of China)

**ILLUS. 6 - GRAVESTONE INSCRIPTIONS, DUAL FAMILY NAME,
COMPOSITE**

WE'RE RELATED, PLEASE FILL OUR A QUESTIONNAIRE!

My name is_____. A photo of my family is enclosed.

I'm tracing our family history. Please fill out this questionnaire and send it
to me at this address:_____.
Your name:_____

Chinese name:_____

Birthdate:_____Birthplace: _____

Occupation:_____Achievements: _____

Information of your mother:

Mother's maiden name:_____Chinese: _____

Birthdate:_____Birthplace:_____
Sibling's name(s) _____ Address(es)_____

Information of your father:

Father's name:_____Chinese:_____
Birthdate:_____Birthplace:_____
Occupation:_____Achievements:_____
Membership in family association. Which?_____
Sibling's name(s) _____ Address(es)_____

When did your first relative immigrate into the U.S.? _____

Name:_____How_____

Date of Arrival: _____ Occupation of relative:_____

Achievements:_____

ILLUS. 7 - FAMILY HISTORY QUESTIONNAIRE

FAMILY RECORD OF _____ _____

                        (Surname of Husband)   (Surname of Wife)

Family Data:

HUSBAND_____ Father _____

born_____ b. _____

wh._____ m. _____

marr._____ d. _____

wh._____ Mother _____

died_____ b. _____

wh._____ d. _____

cem._____

wh_____

WIFE_____ Father _____

born_____ b. _____

wh_____ m. _____

died_____ d. _____

wh_____ Mother _____

cem._____ b. _____

wh._____ d. _____

Children

1._____Born_____ Married   References

                           Died_____ _____ _____

2._____Born_____ Married   References

                           Died_____ _____ _____

3._____Born_____ Married   References

                           Died_____ _____ _____

4._____Born_____ Married   References

                           Died_____ _____ _____

5._____Born_____ Married   References

                           Died_____ _____ _____

6._____Born_____ Married   References

                           Died_____ _____ _____

Compiled by: Address   Date

ILLUS. 8 - FAMILY RECORD

RESOURCES

Angel Island Association: (1-415-435-3522)
Call for large group guided tours of the dormitories. For immigration records, see: National Archives, Pacific Sierra Region.

Angel Island Tour: (1-415-546-2628)
San Francisco Bay, California, Immigration dormitories restored. Audio visual exhibits. Tram to restored dormitories. Biking, hiking, picnicking.

California Genealogy Society Library: 300 Brannan St., S.F. Fee. (1-415-777-9936). U.S. Census. Death records for select states.

California Historical Society, Library: 2099 Pacific Ave., S.F. (1-415-567-1848). Fee charge. Books and photos of old Chinatown.

Chinese Culture Center: 750 Kearny St., S.F. (1-415-986-1822). Gallery and exhibitions. "In Search of Roots Program".

Chinese Historical Society of America, Museum: 650 Commercial St., S.F. 94111. (1-415-391-1188). Exhibits and artifacts. Monthly speakers, workshops.

Church of Latter Day Saints, Family History Center: 4770 Lincoln Ave., Oakland, CA. (1-510-531-3905).

Ellis Island National Monument: New York, New York, 10004. (1-212-363-7620). Museum open 9-5PM. Closed on Christmas. For immigration records, see: Resources: National Archives, Northeast Region.

Eugene C. Barker History Center. Austin, Texas. (1-512-471-5961). Name Index of individuals mentioned in old Texas newspapers.

Family History Center: 975 Sneath Lane, San Bruno, CA. 94066. (415-873-1928).

CHINA CONNECTION

Resources (Cont'd)

Family History Library: 35 North West Temple St., Salt Lake City, Utah 84150. (1-801-240-3796). Interlibrary use available, fee. See Family History Centers in telephone directories. 1500 locations in the world.

Hawaii Chinese History Center: 111 North King St., #410 Honolulu, Hawaii 96817.

Huntington Library: 1151 Oxford Rd., San Marino, CA. (1-818-405-2141). Donation.

Institute for Texas Culture. San Antonio, Texas. (1-512-226-7651). Early years of Chinese in Texas.

National Archives: The case dockets briefly mention case names. On site search of microfiche necessary. Court petition numbers may be obtained by calling district/circuit/or federal court in locale of naturalization.

Generally, records over seventy-five years old are open to the public. For other family records, bring death certificates and petition numbers for documents to be released or send (Freedom of Information and Privacy Act Form G639 to Department of Justice of jurisdictional court.) Privacy Act requests allow for the first 100 pages copied, free. Freedom of Information requests require a fee of $6 for 24 pages; and .25 for each additional copy, if staff at the National Archives fill search-copy requests.

Helpful: *Guide to Records in the National Archives...*each region publication. Washington, D.C.: National Archives and Records Administration, 1989.

Ask to speak to an archivist if telephoning for information regarding records.

National Archives - Alaska Region
654 West Third Avenue
Anchorage, AK 99501
(1-907-271-2441)

Holdings: Alaska

Resources (Cont'd)

National Archives - Central Plains Region
2312 East Bannister Road
Kansas City, MO 64131
(1-816-926-6272)

Holdings: Iowa, Kansas, Missouri, Nebraska

National Archives - Great Lakes Region
7358 South Pulaski Road
Chicago, IL 60629
(1-312-581-7816)

Holdings: Illinois, Indiana, Michigan, Minnesota, Ohio, Wisconsin
1993: Inventory on microfiche.

National Archives - Mid Atlantic Region
9th and Market St., Room 1350
Philadelphia, PA 19107
(1-215-597-3000)

Holdings: Delaware, Maryland, Pennsylvania, Virginia, West Virginia.
1993: Inventory list, 1900-1923; 1895-1920, some to 1952.

National Archives - New England Region
380 Trapelo Road
Waltham, MA 02154
(1-617-647-8100)

Holdings: Connecticut, Maine, Massachusetts, New Hampshire, Rhode
Island, Vermont.

National Archives - Northeast Region
201 Varick Street
New York, NY 10014
(1-212-337-1300)

Resources (Cont'd)

Holdings: New Jersey, New York, Puerto Rico, the Virgin Islands.
1993: Database in progress for Chinese files.

National Archives - Pacific Northwest Region
6125 Sand Point Way NE
Seattle, WA 98115
(1-206-526-6507)

Holdings: Idaho, Oregon, Washington.
1993: Database planned for Chinese files. Availability: Difficult.

National Archives - Pacific Sierra Region
1000 Commodore Drive
San Bruno, CA. 94066
(1-415) 876-9009

Holdings: Northern California, Hawaii, Nevada (except Clark County),
Pacific Trust Territories, American Samoa.
1993: Case Files of Chinese Immigrants to San Francisco and Hawaii.
Index of Philadelphia, PA.

Additional Microfilm: Chinese Mortuary Records for San Francisco
and California, 1870-1933 (English); Certificates of Identity for
Chinese Immigrants, 1909-1946; List of Partnerships; Departure case
files, 1912-1943. Other good sources. (Cabinet 40, Drawer 9).
Availability: Good

National Archives - Pacific Southwest Region
24000 Avila Road
Laguna Niguel, CA. 92656
(1-714-643-4241)

Holdings: Arizona, Southern California, Clark County in Nevada.
1993: No index. Database planned for Chinese. Available of records:
Difficult.

CHINA CONNECTION

Resources (Cont'd)

National Archives - Rocky Mountain Region
Building 48-Denver Federal Center
Denver, CO 80225-0307
(1-303-236-0817)

Holdings: Colorado, Montana, North Dakota, South Dakota, Utah, Wyoming, New Mexico (See Southwest Region *New Mexico).

National Archives - Southeast Region
1557 St. Joseph Avenue
East Point, GA 30344
(1-404-763-7477)

Holdings: Alabama, Florida, Georgia, Kentucky, Mississippi, North Carolina, South Carolina, Tennessee.

National Archives - Southwest Region
501 West Felix Street, P.O. Box 6216
Ft. Worth, TX 76115
(1-817-334-5525)

Holdings: Arkansas, Louisiana, New Mexico*, Oklahoma, Texas (*Most Federal agency records at Rocky Mountain Region).
1993: El Paso records indexed on microfilm. Card index of certificates of naturalization, 1831-1906, Louisiana, 1853-1939, Texas. Microfilm: Actual case files of deportation cases, 1892-1915. Availability: Good, call for appointment to see originals.

San Francisco Chinatown Library: 1135 Powell Street, San Francisco, CA. (1-415-274-0275). Large collection of Chinese in America materials. Map of Guangdong.

San Francisco Licensing Bureau: Tax Collector's Office at City Hall, San Francisco, CA. (1-415-554-6208). Founding date of businesses.

Resources (Cont'd)

San Francisco Main Public Library: Larkin & McAllister Streets, San Francisco, CA. (1-415-557-4567). Collection of old S.F. phone directories. Special Collection Department: 1885 map of Chinatown.

San Francisco Maritime Museum Library: Fort Mason, Building E, San Francisco, CA. (1-415-556-9870). Fee charged for photo of vessel from negative.

San Francisco Recorder's Office: City Hall, Room 167. (1-415-554-4176). Grant Deeds of property.

Sutro Library: 480 Winston Drive, San Francisco, CA. (1-415-731-4477). Early California mortuary records or the *Book of the Dead*. (Chinese not listed). Large genealogy collection of European, California, and Spanish. Large microfilm collection of U.S. city directories from 1861-1935, including London, 1677-1855; U.S. Census records.

U.S. Department of Justice - Immigration and Naturalization Service: 630 Sansome Street, San Francisco, CA. 94111-2280. (1-415-705-4453). Call for Form G639 (Privacy and Freedom of Information Request form). Outside of this jurisdiction, call local district of naturalization.

University of California, Berkeley: Bancroft Library. Archives and Special Collections. (1-510-642-6481). Asian-American Ethnic Studies Library. Wheeler Hall. (1-510-642-2218). Extensive local oral history department.

BIBLIOGRAPHICAL RESOURCES

Chan, Sucheng, *Entry Denied: Exclusion of the Chinese Community in America, 1882-1943.* Philadelphia: Temple University Press, 1991.

Chan, Sucheng, *This Bittersweet Soil: The Chinese in California Agriculture, 1860-1910.* Berkeley: University of California Press, 1986.

Char, Tin-Yuke and Char, Wai Jane, *Chinese Historic Sites and Pioneer Families of the Island of Hawaii.* University of Hawaii Press, 1983.

Char, Tin-Yuke, *The Sandalwood Mountains: Readings and Stories of the Early Chinese in Hawaii.* Honolulu: University of Hawaii Press, 1975

Ching, Frank, *Ancestors: 900 Years in the Life of a Chinese Family.* New York: William Morrow and Co., 1988.

Chinn, Thomas W., *Bridging the Pacific: San Francisco Chinatown and its People.* Chinese Historical Society of America, 1989.

Chun, James H., *The Early Chinese in Punaluu.* Honolulu: Yin Sit Sha, 1983

Cohen, Lucy M., *Chinese in the Post Civil War South: A People Without History.* Baton Rouge: Louisiana State University Press, 1984.

Con, Harry, et al., *From China to Canada: A History of the Chinese Communities in Canada.* Toronto: McClelland and Stewart, 1982.

Cuba Commission, *Chinese Emigration: Report.* Taipei: Ch'eng Wen Publishing Co., 1970 (Original edition: Shanghai: Imperial Maritime Customs Press, 1876).

Dicker, Laverne Mau, *The Chinese in San Francisco: A Pictorial History.* New York: Dover Pub., 1979.

CHINA CONNECTION

Bibliographical Resources (Cont'd)

Dillon, Richard H., *The Hatchet Men: The Story of the Tong Wars in San Francisco's Chinatown.* Sausalito: Comstock Editions, Inc. 1962.

Gillenkirk, Jeff and Motlow, James, *Bitter Melon: Stories from the Last Rural Chinese Town in America.* Seattle: University of Washington Press, 1987.

Glick, Clarence E., *Sojourners and Settlers: Chinese Migrants in Hawaii.* Honolulu: Hawaii Chinese History Center and the University Press of Hawaii, 1980.

Gong, Eng Ying, *Tong War! The First Complete History of the Tongs in America.* New York: Nicolas L. Brown, 1930.

Harvey, Nick. Edited, *Ting: The Caldron, Chinese Art and Identity in San Francisco.* San Francisco: Glide Urban Center, 1970.

Hildebrand, Lorraine Barker, *Straw Hats, Sandals, and Steel: The Chinese in Washington State.* Tacoma: Washington State Historical Society, 1977.

Hom, Gloria Sun, *Chinese Argonauts: An Anthology of the Chinese Contributions to the Historical Development of Santa Clara County.* Santa Clara: Foothill Community College, 1971.

Huck, Arthur, *The Chinese in Australia.* Croydon, Victoria, Australia: Longmans, 1967.

Inman, Bradley, "Chinese Building Legacy in City One of Exclusion". *San Francisco Examiner,* May, 1992.

Kim, Huang-Chan. Edited. *Dictionary of Asian American History.* New York: Greenwood Press, 1986.

Larson, Louise Leung, *Sweet Bamboo: Saga of a Chinese American Family.* Los Angeles: Chinese Historical Society of Southern California, 1989.

CHINA CONNECTION

Bibliographical Resources (Cont'd)

Loewen, James W., *The Mississippi Chinese: Between Black and White.* Cambridge, Massachusetts: Harvard University Press, 1971.

Lowenstein, Louis K., *Streets of San Francisco: The Origins of Streets and Place Names.* San Francisco: Lexikos, 1954.

McCunn, Ruthanne Lum, *Chinese American Portraits: Personal Histories, 1828-1988.* San Francisco: Chronicle Books, 1988.

Mackie, J.A.C., *The Chinese in Indonesia: Five Essays.* Honolulu: University of Hawaii in Association with The Australian Institute of International Affairs, 1976.

Morton, James, *In the Sea of Sterile Mountains: The Chinese in British Columbia.* Vancouver: J.J. Douglas, 1973.

Quan, Robert Seto, *Lotus Among the Magnolias: The Mississippi Chinese.* Jackson, Mississippi: University Press of Mississippi, 1982.

Shang, Anthony, *The Chinese in Britain.* London: Batsford Academic and Educational, 1984.

Siu, Paul C.P., *The Chinese Laundryman: A Study of Social Isolation.* New York: New York University Press, 1987.

Steiner, Stan, *Fusang: The Chinese Who Built America.* San Francisco: Harper & Row Publishers, 1979.

Stewart, Watt, *Chinese Bondage in Peru: A History of the Chinese Coolie in Peru, 1849-1874.* Durham, North Carolina: Duke University Press, 1951.

Yung, Judy, *Chinese Women of America: A Pictorial History.* Seattle: University of Washington, 1986.

BIBLIOGRAPHY

Anonymous, *"Personal Interviews, 1988-1993"*. San Francisco.

Barth, Gunther, *Bitter Strength: A History of the Chinese in the United States, 1850-1870.* Cambridge: Harvard University Press, 1974.

Cather, Helen Virginia, *The History of San Francisco's Chinatown.* San Francisco: R. & E. Associates, [1974] 1932.

The Chinese American Experience: Papers from the Second National Conference on Chinese American Studies. San Francisco: Chinese Historical Society of America and the Chinese Culture Foundation of San Francisco, 1984.

"The Chinese in California, Special Issue", *California History,* Vol,. 57, No. 1, Spring, 1978.

Chinn, Thomas W., "Genealogical Methods and Sources for the Chinese Immigrant to the United States". *Chinese Historical Society of America, Bulletin.* Vol. 4, No. 9, November, 1969.

Chinn, Thomas W., Lai, H. Mark, and Choy, Philip, editors, *A History of the Chinese in California: A Syllabus.* San Francisco: Chinese Historical Society of America, 1973.

Counterpoint: Perspectives on Asian America. Los Angeles: Asian American Studies Center, Resource Development and Publications, University of California, Los Angeles, 1976.

Ginsburg, Marsha, "Push for Center on Angel Island", *San Francisco Examiner,* November 6, 1992.

Guide to Records in the National Archives - Alaska; Central Plains; Great Lakes; Mid Atlantic; New England; Northeast; Northwest; Pacific Sierra; Pacific Southwest; Rocky Mountain; Southeast; and Southwest Regions. Washington D.C.: National Archives and Records Administration, 1989.

CHINA CONNECTION

Bibliography (Cont'd)

Hansen, Gladys, *San Francisco Almanac: Everything You Want To Know About The City*. San Francisco: Chronicle Books, 1975.

Kao, George, *Cathay By The Bay: San Francisco Chinatown In 1950*. Hong Kong: Chinese University Press, 1988.

Kuan, Petra-Haring and Kuan, Yu-Chien, *Magnificent China: A Guide To Its Cultural Treasures*. San Francisco: China Books & Periodicals, Inc., 1988.

Lai, Him Mark, Huang, Joe, and Wong, Don, *The Chinese of America, 1785-1980*. San Francisco: Chinese Culture Foundation, 1980.

Lai, Him Mark, Lim, Genny, and Yung, Judy, *Island: Poetry and History of Chinese Immigration on Angel Island, 1910-1940*. San Francisco: HOC DOI Project, 1980.

McCunn, Ruthanne Lum, *An Illustrated History of Chinese in America*. San Francisco: Design Enterprises of San Francisco, 1979.

Nee, Victor G. and de Bary, Brett, *Longtime Californ': A Documentary Study Of An American Chinatown*. Boston: Houghton Mifflin Co., 1974.

Sandmeyer, Elmer Clarence, *The Anti-Chinese Movement In California*. Chicago: University of Illinois Press, 1973.

Sung, Betty Lee, *The Story of the Chinese in America*. Boston: Houghton Mifflin Co., 1974.

Takaki, Ronald, *Strangers From A Different Shore: A History of Asian Americans*. New York, Penguin Books, 1989.

Tung, William L., *The Chinese in America, 1820-1973: A Chronology And Fact Book*. New York: Oceana Publications, Inc., 1974.

CHINA CONNECTION

Bibliography (Cont'd)

U.S. Department of Labor. Immigration and Naturalization,"Memorandum Concerning Death Records, October 1918-April 30, 1933", Angel Island, CA: 1935

U.S. Department of Labor. Immigration and Naturalization, "Mortuary Records and Indexes of Deaths Occurring Previous to San Francisco Earthquake and Fire of April, 1906", San Francisco: 1915.

Waugh, Dexter, "Chinese Still Can't Forget Island Prison", *San Francisco Examiner,* November 4, 1990.

Wong, H.K., *Gold Mountain Men: Gum Sahn Yun.* San Francisco: Fong Brothers Printing, Inc., 1987.

World Book Encyclopedia. Volume 1-22. Chicago: World Book Inc., 1985.

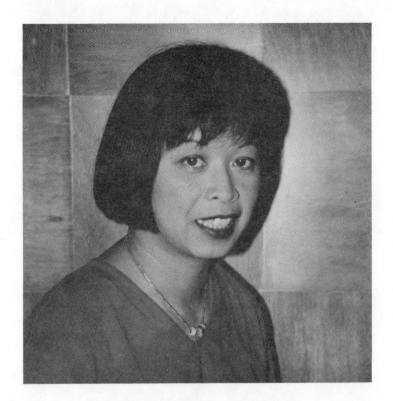

ABOUT THE AUTHOR

Jeanie W. Chooey Low is a second generation Chinese-American and a native San Franciscan. Graduate of Hip Wo Chinese Academy, Elementary Division. Holder: A.A. Degree in Library Technology from City College of San Francisco and a B.A. Degree in Chinese Studies from San Francisco State University. Employed by the University of California, San Francisco Medical Library.

Panelist, "The Repeal and Its Legacy", A Conference on the 50th Anniversary of the Repeal of the Chinese Exclusion Acts, November 12-14, 1993. Sponsored by the Chinese Historical Society of America and Asian American Studies, San Francisco State University.

Jeanie is currently in business management. Member of: Chinese Historical Society of America and the California Genealogy Society.

Formerly, Chinese Methodist Church, Primary teacher; Hip Wo Drum Corp.; and the Flying Eaglettes.